S0-BHW-083

The Countries

Morocco

Bob Italia
ABDO Publishing Company

Published by ABDO Publishing Company, 4940 Viking Drive, Suite 622, Edina, Minnesota 55435.
Copyright © 2000 Abdo Consulting Group, Inc., Pentagon Tower, P.O. Box 36036, Minneapolis,
Minnesota 55435 USA. International copyrights reserved in all countries. No part of this book may be
reproduced in any form without written permission from the publisher.

Printed in the United States.

Editors: Tamara L. Britton, Kate A. Furlong
Art Direction & Maps: Pat Laurel
Cover & Interior Design: MacLean & Tuminelly (Mpls.)
Interior Photos: Corbis

Library of Congress Cataloging-in-Publication Data

Italia, Bob, 1955-
    Morocco / Bob Italia.
        p. cm. -- (The countries)
Includes index.
ISBN 1-57765-393-9
  1. Morocco--Juvenile literature. [1. Morocco.] I. Title. II. Series.

DT305 .I83 2000
964--dc21

00-033214

Contents

Sbah el kheer!

Hello from Morocco! Though it is small, Morocco is rich in **culture** and history.

Morocco was first settled thousands of years ago by the Berbers. Later, Arabs and Europeans settled there. After independence from France, Morocco became a kingdom. One of its kings ruled for 38 years.

Morocco is an African country. But, it is separated from the rest of the continent by mountains and the largest desert in the world.

Agriculture is an important part of Morocco's **economy**. The country also has modern **industries**. But, crafts are what made Morocco famous.

There are many modern cities in Morocco. Fez is famous for its blue pottery. Rabat is Morocco's political capital. Casablanca is the country's largest city. All have ancient sections and markets.

Islam is an important part of Moroccan lives. Religious holidays are observed for two working days. They are filled with dancing, music, and feasts. Festivals are dedicated to popular art and **tradition**.

Moroccans enjoy all types of sports. Some of the most popular are waterskiing, surfing, and motor sports. Moroccans take great pride in their national soccer team.

Morocco is a country with much to offer. It is a country of forests and deserts. It has modern and traditional **cultures**. It also has ties to Arab, European, and African nations. Because of these ties, Morocco plays an important role in the world community.

Sbah el kheer *from Morocco!*

Fast Facts

OFFICIAL NAME: Kingdom of Morocco

CAPITAL: Rabat

LAND
- Area: 172,413 square miles (446,550 sq km)
- Mountain Ranges: Rif, Middle Atlas, High Atlas, and Anti-Atlas
- Highest Point: Jebel Toubkal 13,665 feet (4,165 m)
- Lowest Point: Sea level
- Major Rivers: Moulouya, Sebou
- Deserts: Sahara

PEOPLE
- Population: 29,661,636 (1999 est.)
- Major Cities: Casablanca, Rabat, Fez, Marrakesh
- Major Languages: Arabic (official), Berber dialects, French, Spanish
- Religion: Islam (official)

GOVERNMENT
- Form: Constitutional Monarchy
- Head: King
- Legislature: Chamber of Representatives
- Flag: Red with a green pentacle (five-pointed, linear star) known as Solomon's Seal in the center of the flag; green is the traditional color of Islam
- National Anthem: "*al-Mamlaka al-Maghrebia*"
- Nationhood: March 2, 1956

ECONOMY
- Agricultural Products: Barley, wheat, citrus, wine, vegetables, olives, livestock
- Mining Products: Phosphate rock
- Manufactured Products: Food, leather goods, textiles
- Money: Dirham (one dirham equals one hundred centimes)

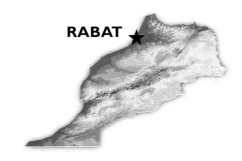

RABAT

Morocco's Flag

A ten-dirham note

Timeline

3000 B.C.	Berbers settle in North Africa
1200 B.C.	Phoenicians invade Morocco
146 B.C.	Rome controls Morocco
A.D. 600s	Arabs control Morocco
788	Idrissid Dynasty established
1055	Almoravid Dynasty begins
1130	Almohad Dynasty takes control
1258	Merinides Dynasty begins
1400s	Spain and Portugal invade Morocco
1520	Saadian Dynasty established
1578	Battle of the Three Kings
1660	Alaouite Dynasty begins
1800s	European powers battle for control of Morocco
1911	France and Spain rule Morocco
1927	Mohammed V takes the throne
1953	Mohammed V sent to Madagascar
1956	Morocco gains independence
1961	Mohammed V dies; Hassan II gains the throne
1975	The Green March to the Moroccan Sahara
1999	King Hassan II dies; King Mohammed VI takes the throne

Ancient History

Morocco's history began with the Berbers. They lived in North Africa as early as 3000 B.C.

The first invaders were the Phoenicians. They came from Caanan in the Eastern Mediterranean in 1200 B.C. Slowly, they built trading posts along the north coast of Africa.

The **Carthaginians** turned the north coast settlements into prosperous towns. Rome took control of Morocco after defeating Carthage in 146 B.C.

As the Roman Empire fell, the Vandals invaded Morocco. In the seventh century, the Arabs took control. They ruled for more than a century.

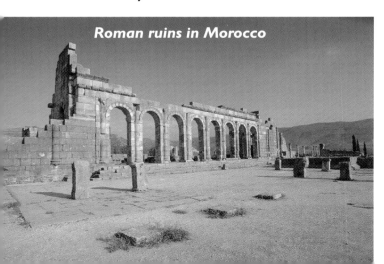
Roman ruins in Morocco

From the 800s to the 1300s, different **dynasties** came to power. They included the Idrissids, Almoravids, and Almohads. None kept the support of the Berber leaders.

By the fifteenth century, Spain and Portugal began to invade Morocco. In 1415, the Portuguese captured the Moroccan port of Ceuta. In 1578, Morocco defeated the Portuguese forces in the Battle of the Three Kings.

The latest Moroccan **dynasty**, the Alaouite, came to power in 1660. By 1700, Morocco had regained control of many coastal towns captured by the Portuguese. But, by the middle of the nineteenth century, the European powers had become too great. They fought each other for control of Morocco.

Sultan Mohammed V (right) with General Francisco Franco of Spain

By 1911, France ruled most of Morocco. Spain controlled a smaller part. Mohammed V took the throne in 1927 and became Morocco's **sultan**. The French hoped to easily control him. But, Mohammed V supported Moroccan rights and independence.

King Hassan II

After World War II, Morocco's independence movement grew. In 1950, Mohammed V requested self-government. The French said no. In 1953, the **sultan** was sent to Madagascar. But, he was allowed to return two years later.

France did not grant Morocco independence until 1956. A year later, Mohammed V became king of Morocco. At the same time, Spain gave up most of its Moroccan land. They kept only a few cities and territories.

In 1961, King Mohammed V died. His son, Crown Prince Hassan II, took the throne. For 38 years, King Hassan II ruled the country. He survived many attempts to overthrow him. Hassan's leadership had Morocco headed toward **economic** prosperity.

In 1975, more than 350,000 unarmed Moroccans marched into the Moroccan Sahara. They protested Spain's control of this land and claimed it for Morocco. The protest was called the Green

March. Morocco still claims ownership of the Moroccan Sahara. But, many nations recognize the land as the independent country of Western Sahara.

On July 23, 1999, King Hassan II died at the age of 70. His death marked an end of an **era**. He was one of the longest serving kings in the modern history of the Arab world.

That same day, the king's son, crown prince Mohammed Ibn Al Hassan, took the throne as King Mohammed VI. He became the eighteenth king in the Alaouite **dynasty**.

Hassan II's death created uncertainty for the young Moroccan nation. But, Morocco now plays an important role in the dealings among African, Arab, and European countries.

King Mohammed VI

The Land

A valley in the Rif Mountains

Morocco is located on the northwestern corner of Africa. Algeria is to its east and southeast. Western Sahara is to its south. The Atlantic Ocean is to Morocco's west. And, the Mediterranean Sea is to its north.

Morocco is divided into three natural regions. The fertile northern coastal plain along the Mediterranean contains the Rif Mountains. They rise to about 8,000 feet (2,438 m). The **plateaus** and lowlands lie between

Detail
Area

the Atlas Mountains and the Mediterranean Sea. The dry area in southern and eastern Morocco runs into the Sahara Desert.

The Atlas Mountains

Morocco has four separate mountain ranges. Three run alongside each other from the southwest to the northeast. They are the Middle Atlas, the High Atlas, and the Anti-Atlas.

The Atlas Mountains have an average height of 11,000 feet (3,353 m). They contain some of the highest peaks in North Africa. At 13,665 feet (4,165 m), Jebel Toubkal is the highest peak. South of the Atlas lie the Anti-Atlas Mountains. The volcanic Mt. Siroua at 10,840 feet (3,304 m) is found there.

Mt. Jebel Toubkal

Morocco has North Africa's largest river system. Most Moroccan rivers flow northwest to the Atlantic or southeast to the Sahara. But, the Moulouya flows 350 miles (563 km) northeast from the Atlas to the Mediterranean Sea.

The main rivers that flow into the Atlantic are the Oumer, Sebou, Bou Regreg, Tensift, Draa, and Sous. The Ziz and Gheris are the main rivers flowing south toward the Sahara.

The Sahara Desert in Morocco

The Moroccan coastline runs along the Mediterranean Sea and the Atlantic Ocean. It has many beaches and old coastal cities.

In the southeast, Morocco's mountain ranges end at the Sahara Desert. The rivers that flow down this side of the High Atlas form long, narrow, and lush valleys.

Morocco's climate is mostly dry. The rainy seasons are from October to November and from April to May. The most rainfall occurs in the northwest.

Morocco also has many temperature ranges. The southern and southeastern desert regions are hot during the summer. In the mountains, it is cool in summer and freezing in winter. The early summer months are the most comfortable. There is little rain. Temperatures are warm during the day and cool at night.

Rainfall

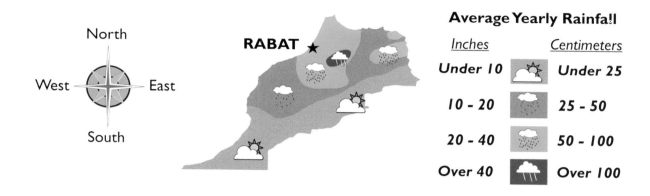

Average Yearly Rainfall

Inches		*Centimeters*
Under 10		*Under 25*
10 - 20		*25 - 50*
20 - 40		*50 - 100*
Over 40		*Over 100*

Temperature

Winter

Summer

AVERAGE TEMPERATURE

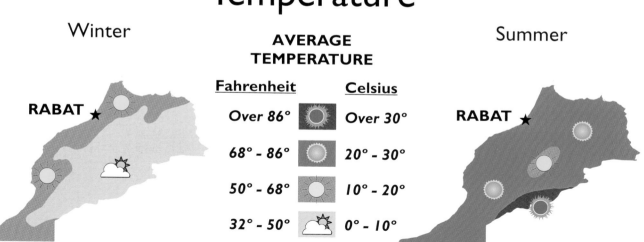

Fahrenheit		**Celsius**
Over 86°		*Over 30°*
68° - 86°		*20° - 30°*
50° - 68°		*10° - 20°*
32° - 50°		*0° - 10°*

Plants & Animals

Morocco's mountain regions contain large forests. In the lower regions, there are large stands of cork oak, evergreen oak, and juniper. Cedar, fir, and pine grow in the higher regions.

Scrub brush and grass usually cover the plains. On the plain of Sous, near the southern border, is a large forest of argan. They are thorny trees found mostly in Morocco.

Morocco has many kinds of wildlife. The most common are the gazelle, wild boar, panther, wild goat, baboon, fox, rabbit, otter, squirrel, and horned viper.

Cork oaks in Morocco

An argan tree

Baboons are 20 to 45 inches (50 to 115 cm) long without the tail. They have large fangs and powerful limbs. Baboons are often found on the ground and in the trees of dry grasslands.

Gazelles stand 2 to 3 feet high (60 to 90 cm) at the shoulder. They are found on open plains and near deserts.

Horned vipers have long, hollow fangs which they use to inject poison into their prey. They are found in sandy deserts. The adult is only 18 to 28 inches (45 to 70 cm) long. It has a broad, triangular head with a sharp, upright scale above each eye that looks like a horn.

Berbers & Others

A Berber woman

The largest group of peoples in Morocco is the Berbers. They are a native, northwest African, non-Arab, **tribal** people. Sanhaja, Masmoda, and Zenata are the three Berber tribes. They live in large areas of Morocco, Algeria, and Tunisia. The Berber language has almost 300 different **dialects**.

Some historians think the Berbers are a mix of European and Asian peoples. The name Berbers was given to them by the Arabs. It means "those who were not Arabs."

Over the centuries, the Berbers slowly became part of the Arab **culture**. Most still live in the country's **rural** areas. They raise livestock and grow crops. The Berbers are also found in many other **traditional** and modern jobs.

Arabs are Morocco's second-largest group. They came to Morocco during the Muslim conquests in the seventh century A.D. Most live in the cities. There is also a small population of people of African **descent**. And, there's a European community of about 100,000. Most are French.

Arabic is Morocco's official language. Most Moroccans speak it. French is a common second language in the cities. Spanish is the second language of many people in the northern cities.

Most Moroccans are Muslim. They follow the teachings of **Islam**. Others are Jewish or Christian.

In Morocco, there are many different kinds of clothing. People in **rural** areas wear traditional dress. People in the city often wear European clothes.

The *kaftan* is a woven, floor-length garment that comes in many colors. Women wear *kaftans* with or without a veil.

A southern Moroccan woman in traditional dress

The women of the High Atlas wear layers of colorful clothing to stay warm. They also wear silver jewelry and head scarfs.

Southern Moroccan women often wear layers of black or blue material draped around them and over their heads. Northern Moroccan women often wear the **traditional** *fouta*. It is a piece of white material with red, blue, or black stripes worn as a skirt.

Men wear a *burnous*. It is a circular cloak with a large square hood, over a belted tunic. On their feet are *babouche*, Moroccan slipper shoes. The men from Tafraoute are known as the Blue Men because they wrap themselves in blue material. They wear a *chesch* on their heads.

Traditional Berber clothes include the *djellaba*. It is the tunic that men layer over other light clothing. In the south, a *chesch* covers the ears to protect them in the desert.

Moroccan boys and girls between 7 and 13 years old must go to school. There is a nine-year fundamental education period and a three-year secondary education period. Secondary education helps 16- to 18-year-old students carry on their studies in general or technical education.

Moroccans live in different types of homes. **Villas**, or modern homes with gardens, are often found in the cities. There are also much smaller homes with flat roofs. Most face into a small, central courtyard.

Kasbahs are in **rural** areas. They are buildings made of palm-tree fibers and mud-

A Moroccan classroom

clay bricks. Some villages are carved into the mountainsides. Others have small groups of whitewashed houses with small windows covered with iron grilles. **Nomads** live in black tents in desert areas and mountain valleys.

A village of mud-brick homes

Coconut Cakes

Moroccan coconut cakes are a delicious treat much like coconut fudge. They are easy to make and are an ideal dessert.

In a 2-quart saucepan, combine 2 cups grated coconut (moist, canned, or fresh), 3/4 cup of evaporated milk, and 2 cups sugar. Simmer gently until a soft ball is formed in cold water. Add 1 oz. butter and 2 tbs. lemon rind. Cool to room temperature in the pan. Beat as you would fudge until thick and glossy. Pour into an 8 x 8-inch (20 x 20-cm) pan lined with wax paper. Chill and cut into squares. Makes 1 1/2 pounds (1 kg) of coconut fudge.

AN IMPORTANT NOTE TO THE CHEF: Always have an adult help with the preparation and cooking of food. Never use kitchen utensils or appliances without adult permission and supervision.

Crafting an Economy

Agriculture is an important part of Morocco's **economy**. The main crops are sugarcane, sugar beets, wheat, barley, tomatoes, potatoes, oranges, melons, olives, grapes, **pulses**, and dates. Moroccans also raise sheep, goats, and cattle.

Cork is also produced in Morocco. Timber is cut from forests in the Rif and Atlas regions.

Fishing is another important part of the economy. Most fish come from Atlantic port cities such as Casablanca, Agadir, Safi, and Essaouira. Morocco is a leading supplier of sardines.

Phosphate is Morocco's main mineral **resource**. Other mineral resources include coal, iron ore, lead, manganese, and zinc.

Morocco's factories produce chemicals, textiles, construction materials, footwear, processed foods, wine, refined petroleum, and other products.

A Moroccan phosphate mine

Crafts are Morocco's most famous product. Handwoven and **embroidered** cloth, leatherwork, **ceramics**, woodwork, and carpets are made by **artisans** throughout the country. Morocco's crafts are now sold throughout the world. Morocco's main trading partners are France, Spain, Italy, Germany, the United States, and the United Arab Emirates.

Carpets for sale at a Moroccan market

Morocco has 12 daily national newspapers and many magazines. The international London-based Arabic daily *Asharq Alawsat* is also printed in Morocco.

There are many radio channels that can be heard in several languages. The state television has programming in Arabic, English, and French. An Arabsat satellite channel broadcasts across North Africa and the Middle East.

Morocco has one of Africa's largest **telecommunications** networks. Most of it is run by the National Posts and Telecommunication Board (O.N.P.T.), a government institution. Privately-owned telecommunication services are also available.

New Old Cities

Nearly all Moroccan cities have three parts: the *medina*, the modern town, and the *souk*.

The *medinas* are older sections with narrow, winding streets. Arabs built the *medinas* during **medieval** times. The modern towns have newer homes and **villas**. The French built them outside the *medinas*. *Souks* are crowded market areas filled with tiny shops. They are often found inside the *medinas*.

Casablanca's port

Casablanca is Morocco's largest city and business capital. It is also one of North Africa's most important commercial centers. More than half of all Moroccan companies and almost every bank is located there. Casablanca produces construction materials, furniture, and glass products.

Casablanca is the country's main Atlantic seaport. It has one of the world's largest man-made harbors.

Hassan II Mosque

Casablanca is home to one of the world's largest **mosques**. The Hassan II Mosque covers 4.9 acres (2 ha). It has a prayer hall that can hold 25,000 worshippers. It also has a **piazza** that can hold another 80,000. The Mosque has the world's tallest **minaret**, soaring 656 feet (200 m) above the city.

Rabat is on Morocco's Atlantic coastline and at the mouth of Bou Regreg River. It is Morocco's capital. It is also the king's official home. All **ministries** and **embassies** are located in Rabat.

Rabat was founded as an Arab army outpost in the twelfth century. Its name means "military camp." The outpost is still used today.

Rabat is also one of the country's main **industrial** centers. Textiles, processed food, and building materials are manufactured there. The city also contains several of Morocco's major educational institutions.

The city of Fez

Across the Bou Regreg River from Rabat lies the town of Salé. Rabat and Salé are sister cities. A bridge across the river connects them. Salé has many industries including fish canning, cork processing, ceramics, flour milling, and carpet weaving. The Rabat-Salé **urban** area is Morocco's second-largest.

Fez is famous for its blue pottery. It is known as *Fakhari* by the locals and *Bleu de Fez* by the French. Fez is also known for its leather goods, woolen carpets, carved wood, and gold, brass, and silver objects.

Fez is located in a valley that provides the basic materials for its pottery. Clay is dug from the hills at Ben Jelleih, 7 miles (11 km) east of Fez.

Fez is home to the tomb of Moulay Idris II. It is one of Morocco's most holy places. Non-Muslims may not enter or approach the entrance. Fez also has one of the largest **mosques** in Africa, the Qarawiyyin Mosque.

Marrakech is an **oasis** on the Haouz Plain at the foot of the High Atlas Mountains. The city was founded in 1062 as the capital of the Almoravid **dynasty**.

Marrakech is a rail center for other parts of Morocco. Roads link the city with the north and with the Atlantic seaport of Safi.

Local **industries** include tanning and crafts. Marrakech is famous for its leatherwork and desert carpets. Lead, zinc, copper, molybdenum, and graphite are mined nearby.

Tangier has been called the Gateway to Morocco. King Hassan II used it as the country's summer capital. Tangier overlooks the Strait of Gibraltar. Spanish tourists like to travel there.

Tangier is also known for the Mendoubia gardens. It has 800-year-old trees. Tangier's Kasbah Square is another famous landmark. It has a **portico** of white marble columns, which adds to Tangier's fame as the "White City."

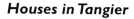

Houses in Tangier

Trains, Planes & Buses

Morocco has a 36,786-mile (59,198-km) network of paved roads. They extend throughout the country, even into the Sahara. Moroccans drive on the right-hand side of the roads.

Ferries operate from Algeciras, Malaga, and Almeria in Spain; from Sete in France; and from Gibraltar.

The country has a railway system with 1,907 miles (3,068 km) of track. It runs mostly in the north, and links all the main towns. The service is modern, comfortable, and fast. Morocco also has intercity train service with 669,637 passenger cars.

A train on the Morocco-Tangier railway

Royal Air Maroc is the national airline. It flies to Moroccan cities and other countries. Many foreign airlines serve Morocco, including Air France, British Airways, and Saudia, the national airline of Saudi Arabia.

A Royal Air Maroc plane

CTM LN is the main bus company. It links all the main cities. Smaller companies operate regionally. Buses travel throughout the country.

In the cities, *Petit Taxis* are a popular form of transport. *Grands Taxis* carry up to six people and cover **rural** areas, linking towns together. Poor people use donkeys and mules to travel.

Petit Taxis *in Casablanca*

The Kingdom

After gaining independence from France, Morocco became a royal kingdom with a constitutional **monarchy**.

The king acts as head of state and commander in chief of the armed forces. He appoints the country's **prime minister** and **cabinet**.

Morocco's **parliament** has a 306-member Chamber of Representatives. Representatives for 206 seats are elected by the people. Political and **economic** groups choose the remaining 100 representatives.

Morocco has a multi-**party** political system. The main parties are the Istiqlal Party, the Popular Movement, the National Rally of Independents, and the Constitution Union.

The Supreme Court is Morocco's highest **judicial** authority. It is appointed by the king, and is located in the capital.

Morocco is divided into **provinces** and **prefectures**. The king appoints the provincial governors. They answer to the central government.

The Moroccan currency is the *dirham*. It is divided into 100 *centimes*.

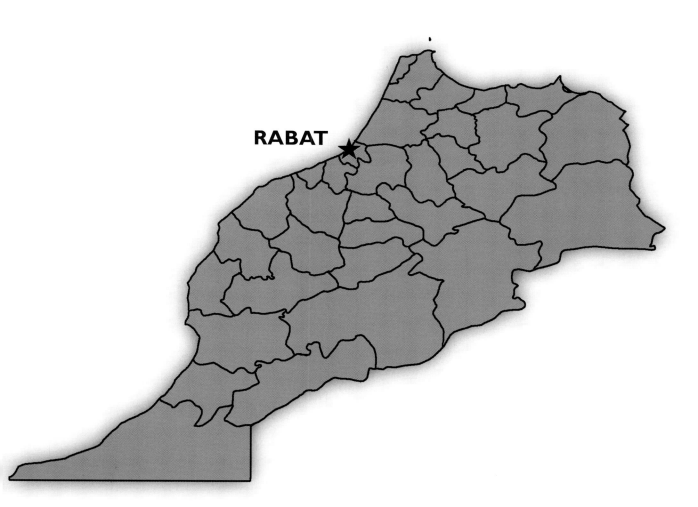

The provinces and prefectures of Morocco

Holidays & Festivals

Religious holidays are celebrated for two working days. They are based on the **lunar calendar**. So, their dates are fixed after the moon cycles and change each year.

Aid es Seghir (ah-EED es-say-GEER) marks the end of Ramadan, the month of **fasting**. The celebration begins on the first day of the tenth moon. People wear new clothing. They exchange gifts with children or friends.

Aid el Kebir (ah-EED el-kay-BEER) recalls the biblical figure Abraham and his willingness to sacrifice his son, Isaac. The holiday begins on the tenth day of the twelfth moon. Every family offers a ram or other animal. Its meat is shared with relatives, friends, neighbors, and the poor. There's also music and dancing.

Muharram (mo-HAH-ram) is the New Year celebration. It is celebrated on the first day of the first moon. People exchange good wishes and lucky pennies. Feasts, music, and dancing occur.

Mouloud (moo-LOOD) celebrates the birthday of the **prophet** Mohammed, the founder of Islam. It falls on the eleventh day of the third moon. There's plenty of music, dancing, and feasts.

The most important state holiday is the Festival of the Throne. It falls on March 3 of every year. It marks the king's rise to the throne. There are fireworks, parades, music, and dancing.

Moussems are large gatherings that honor local holy men. There, you can see fantasias, dances, singing, and **traditional** costume. You can also join the processions and feasts. These events depend upon local **harvests** or the **lunar calendar**.

Asilah is the center of one of Africa's most important artistic festivals. Writers, poets, and artists from all over the Arab and African world attend each year in August.

Moroccan horsemen ride at a hard gallop and then fire their rifles in a fantasia, a traditional Moroccan event.

Sports & Leisure

Every kind of water sport can be found on Morocco's Atlantic and Mediterranean coasts. There is surfing, windsurfing, sailing, yachting, canoeing, rowing, waterskiing, scuba diving, and deep sea fishing.

Soccer was introduced into the region by French **colonists**. In 1970, Morocco was the first African country to play in the World Cup. It was absent from World Cup finals until 1986. That year, it reached the quarterfinals—a first for African soccer.

Morocco's 1998 World Cup team

Motoring is popular in Morocco. It has one of Africa's best road networks. Morocco hosts some of the greatest international competitions, including the Paris-Dakar and Atlas Rallies. There are thousands of miles of roads, giving racing fans a

A car races in the Paris-Dakar Rally.

wide selection of challenges.

There are several rowing clubs along the Atlantic coast, particularly in Rabat, Casablanca, and Kenitra. These clubs hold **regattas** watched by large crowds.

Another popular sport is water skiing. Some Moroccans ski from Mohammedia to Casablanca, or cross the Strait of Gibraltar. The leading ski clubs are on the Atlantic coast.

In Morocco, you can surf all year long. Americans and Australians brought the sport to Morocco in the 1970s. Now, surfing has grown in popularity. There are several organizations that promote surfing. They organize tournaments, contests, and surfing schools.

Morocco is rich in museums overflowing with treasures. Carpets, pottery, garments, arms, and paintings can be viewed. But, **Islamic** teachings forbid representing humans or animals. So, most of Morocco's art is decorated with **geometric** shapes.

Jellabas *for sale in a Marrakesh market*

The *souk,* or market, is a big part of Moroccan life. Since most Moroccans live in **rural** areas, each tribe has a certain number of *souks*. They are often held out in the open country. *Souks* are named after the days of the week on which they are held.

On the day of the *souk*, people erect tents early in the morning. Soon, they are full of brightly-colored clothes, *burnouses*, *jellabas*, **embroidered** gowns, *baboosh* slippers, tea, and spices. Goods are bought, sold, and traded all day. You'll also find storytellers and fortune tellers.

The *souk* allows tourists to mingle with Moroccan **peasants**. Visitors can see how they live, and buy low-cost crafts.

Folk music is the most important kind of Moroccan music. There are many forms of folk music. Most are sung in the Berber or Arabic languages.

Folk music has two parts: chanting and singing, and dancing. Each time people gather to sing, they form a line or a circle. Then, they start to dance to the rhythm of their songs.

The music of the *Gnawa* is folk music from the south Sahara beyond Morocco. It has a clear, balanced rhythm. The music is played on a *sintir*, a three-stringed, skin-faced lute. Drums and metal double castanets accompany the *sintir*. The *Gnawa* are often found in Marrakech. They perform **acrobatic** dances to large audiences in *Place Djemaa el Fna*. It is the city's main market.

Andalusian music is from the Arabs. This classical music can be played by an orchestra. Al Malhoun is a poetic style of music developed from Andalusian music. It started in Fez and became popular in Marrakech.

Morocco owes its rich **culture** to its stormy past. Because of its past, Morocco has become one of Africa's most politically important countries.

Place Djemaa el Fna

Glossary

acrobat - a person who can swing on a trapeze, turn handsprings, walk a tightrope, or perform other feats of bodily skill and strength.

artisan - a person skilled in a craft or trade.

cabinet - a group of advisors chosen by a nation's leader to direct government departments.

Carthaginians - peoples from Carthage, an ancient city-state on the coast of North Africa and northeast of modern Tunis.

ceramic - of pottery or porcelain.

colonist - a person who lives in a colony; a settler.

culture - the customs, arts, and tools of a nation or people at a certain time.

descent - a family line; ancestors.

dialect - a form of a language spoken in a certain area or by a certain group of people.

dynasty - a series of rulers who belong to the same family.

economy - the way a country manages its resources.

embassy - the home and offices of an ambassador and his or her assistants in a foreign country.

embroider - to decorate cloth or leather with a pattern of stitches.

era - a period of time or history.

fast - to go without food.

geometric - made up of straight lines, circles, and other simple shapes.

harvest - a reaping and gathering of food crops.

industry - any form of business, manufacture, or trade.

Islam - the religion based on the teachings of the prophet Mohammed as they appear in the Koran.

judicial - having something to do with a court of law or the administration of justice.

lunar calendar - a calendar based on the phases of the moon.

medieval - of or belonging to the Middle Ages (A.D. 500 to 1450).

minaret - a slender, high tower attached to a Muslim mosque with one or more projecting balconies.

ministry - the office, duties, or time of service of a minister.

monarchy - a government by a king, queen, emperor, or other ruler.

mosque - a Muslim place of worship.

nomad - a member of a tribe which moves from place to place to have food or pasture for its cattle.

oasis - a place in the desert where there is water and where trees and plants can grow.

parliament - a group of persons that has the duty and power to make laws for a state or country.
party - a group of people organized to gain political power.
peasant - a farmer of the working class.
piazza - a large porch along one or more sides of a house.
plateau - flatland in the mountains or high above sea level.
portico - a roof supported by columns, forming a porch or a covered walk.
prefecture - the district governed by a prefect (chief officer).
prime minister - the highest-ranked member of a government.
prophet - a religous leader that speaks the word of God.
province - one of the main divisions of a country.
pulse - the edible seeds of peas, beans, lentils, and similar plants having pods.
regatta - a boat race or a series of boat races.
resource - the actual and possible wealth of a country.
rural - out in the country, not in the city.
sultan - the ruler of certain Muslim countries.
telecommunication - the science or study of sending messages over long distances by electronic means, as by telegraph, telephone, or television.
tradition - the handing down of beliefs, customs, and stories from parents to children.
tribal - characteristic of a tribe.
urban - of or having something to do with cities or towns.
villa - a large, expensive house located in the country, on the edge of a city, or at the seashore.

LANGUAGE

ENGLISH	ARABIC
Thank You _____	Shokran
Hello _____	Sbah el kheer
Goodbye _____	Bisalama
Please _____	Minfadlek
Yes _____	Naam, aiwa
No _____	La

Web Sites

Welcome to Morocco, hosted by the Moroccan Ministry of Communication:
http://www.mincom.gov.ma/english/e_page.html

ArabNet--Morocco: **http://www.arab.net/morocco/morocco_contents.html**

These sites are subject to change. Go to your favorite search engine and type in "Morocco" for more sites.

Index